When Fear Takes Over!
A Practical Guide to Understanding Your Anxiety and Reclaiming Control of Your Life

Dr. Alphonse Semsch

When Fear Takes Over!
A Guide to Understanding Your Anxiety and Taking Back Control

Written by Dr. Alphonse Semsch ™ 2025 by TEXMERALCOR HEALTH AND RESEARCH GROUP, LLC, Austin, Texas

No part of this book may be reproduced, distributed, or transmitted in any form or by any means, including photocopying, recording, or other electronic or mechanical methods, without the prior written permission of the publisher, except in the case of brief quotations embodied in critical reviews and certain other noncommercial uses permitted by copyright law. For permission requests, write to the publisher at the address above.

Library of Congress Control Number (LCCN):
ISBN (Paperback): 979-8-9940038-2-4
ISBN (eBook): 979-8-9940038-3-1

Printed in the United States of America
First Edition: December 2025

This book is not intended to replace professional medical, psychological, or psychiatric advice, diagnosis, or treatment. Always seek the advice of your physician or qualified mental health provider with any questions you may have regarding a medical or psychological condition. Never disregard professional advice or delay in seeking it because of something you have read in this book.

The names, characters, and anecdotes in the testimonial sections are based on real experiences but have been anonymized and modified to protect privacy. Any resemblance to actual persons, living or deceased, is coincidental or used with permission.

Trademark Notice:
"Dr. Alphonse Semsch" is a trademark of TEXMERALCOR HEALTH AND RESEARCH GROUP, LLC.

When Fear Takes Over!
A Practical Guide to Understanding Your Anxiety and Reclaiming Control of Your Life

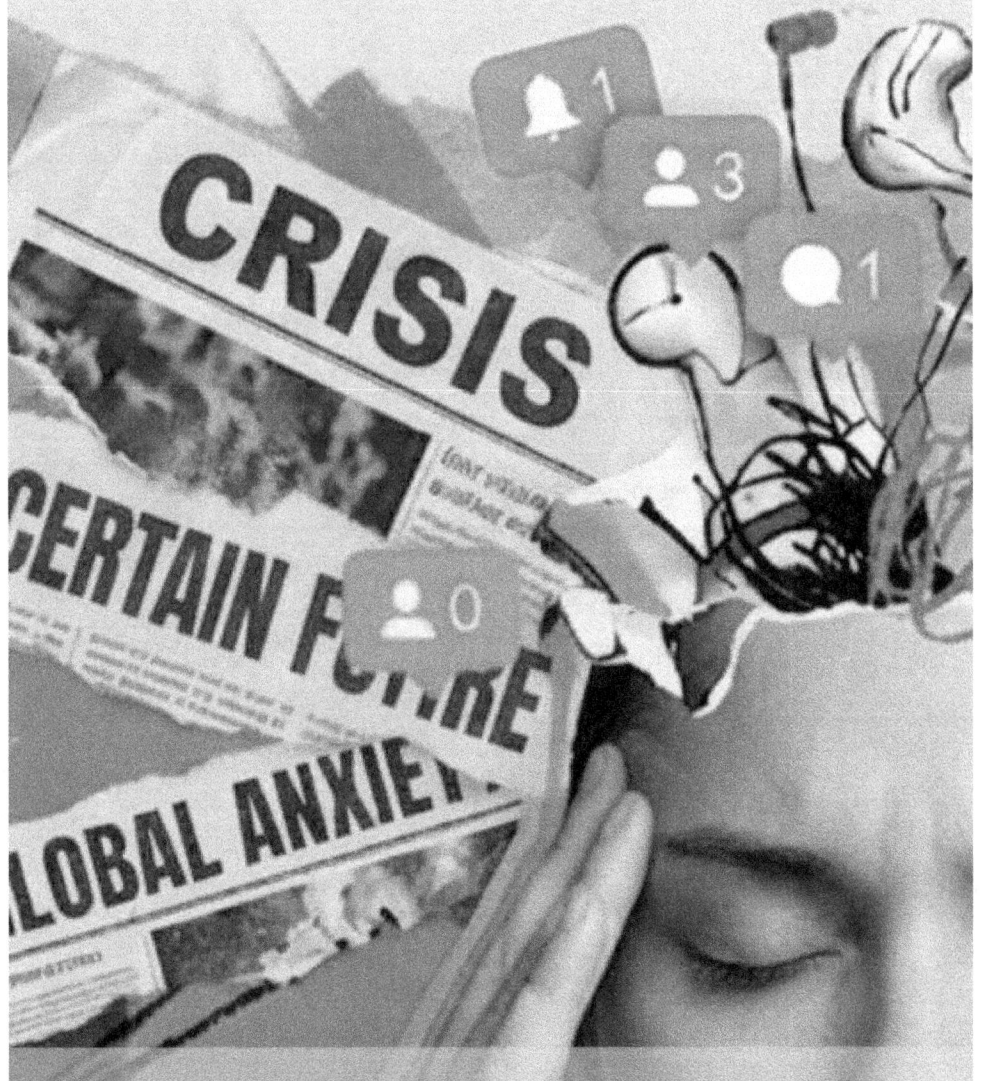

Dr. Alphonse Semsch

To Andrew, my tomodachi,
a friend who walks with me in light and shadow,
who never judges my silences nor demands my victories.

And to all who have carried fear with them
since they were children too small to understand it,
and who, despite everything,
chose to become doctors,
researchers,
caregivers to the pain of others… even while their own still lingers.

This book is not for those who have already conquered anxiety.
It is for those who, like you and like me,
continue to fight day by day… and still, choose to reach out a hand.

— Dr. Alphonse Semsch

Acknowledgments.

To God, the Great Chief of the universe, who needs no intermediaries to listen to a broken heart or accompany a mind in flames. Thank you for the silences that speak, for the signs along the way, and for reminding me, time and again, that purpose is not found in calm, but in navigating the storm with faith.

To my wife, my favorite doctor, my co-author in life. You not only reviewed every paragraph—you lived every chapter by my side. Your science heals bodies; your love heals souls. This book bears your logo because it bears your essence. You are my most accurate diagnosis: "For all of life."

To my children, the light of my days. You are the reason a father strives to be better, stronger, and more present. Thank you for your patience when Dad was "in book mode," and for reminding me, through your laughter, that the best therapy is a wordless hug.

To my teachers and mentors—those in white coats and those with no title but life itself. To those who taught me to listen to the heart, and to those who showed me that sometimes what hurts the most makes no sound in the stethoscope.

To my patients, my greatest teachers: you taught me that anxiety is not an enemy—it is a sign that the soul still fights to live.

And finally, thank you to you, reader, for daring to open this book when the world told you, "Be quiet." "Smile." "Keep going."

You are not alone. And if this book has walked with you for even a little while… that is enough.

Dr. Alphonse Semsch
Under the wide Texas sky, December 2025

Table of contents	Page
"Why This Book Is Not Another Anxiety Manual"	1
BOOK 1: "WHEN FEAR TAKES OVER" *A Practical Guide to Understanding Your Anxiety and Taking Back Control of Your Life*	3
PART 1: Understanding What's Happening to You (Without the Fluff)	4
Chapter 1: "You're Not Crazy, You're Wounded"	5
Quick Access Guide – Chapter 1	7
Chapter 2: "Worrying Is Not the Same as Drowning in 'What If'"	9
Quick Access Guide – Chapter 2	11
Chapter 3: "When Anxiety Becomes Your Toxic 'Friend'"	12
Quick Access Guide – Chapter 3	14
PART 2: Your Basic Toolbox	16
Chapter 4: "Breathing Is Not Optional"	17
Quick Access Guide – Chapter 4	19
Chapter 5: "For the Loop-Playing Mind" (Ruminating Thoughts)	21
Quick Access Guide – Chapter 5	23
Chapter 6: "The Power of a Minimal Routine"	24
Quick Access Guide – Chapter 6	26
Chapter 7: "When to Seek Professional Help?"	27
Quick Access Guide – Chapter 7	29
PART 3: How to Support Someone You Love	31
Chapter 8: "What to Say (and What NOT to Say)"	32
Quick Access Guide – Chapter 8	34
Capítulo 9: "Recursos y líneas de crisis"	36
Quick Access Guide – Chapter 9	39
EPILOGUE: "When Fear Is No Longer in Charge… You Start Living Again"	40
"Your Voice Counts Too!" *Write your own notes, reflections, intentions, or prayers*	42
Bibliography by Chapter	44
About the Author	50

"Why This Book Is Not Another Anxiety Manual"

Forty-seven years ago, in a humble home, an eight-year-old boy sat on the edge of his bed each night, counting the cracks in the ceiling so he wouldn't think about what might happen the next day. *What if I mess up? What if I'm rejected? What if I'm not enough?*

That boy was me.

For years, I believed my anxiety was a curse. I was told: "You're too sensitive," "You overthink everything," "You need to be stronger." And in silence, I felt ashamed. Because while my friends played without fear, I calculated every step: *What if I fall? What if they laugh? What if I'm not enough?*

Over time, I learned to disguise fear as perfection. I studied medicine out of passion—and because I believed that if I could become "the best," maybe the fear would quiet down. But it didn't. It only grew quieter... and heavier.

As a doctor, I felt I had to be a refuge for my patients... even on those nights on call, when I sat alone in the emergency room, heart racing, repeating silently: *Breathe. Just breathe. No one knows you're about to fall apart.*

It was in that moment that I understood something that would change my life: I don't have to overcome anxiety to help others. I only need to walk beside them... with my own wounds visible.

This book was not born in an ivory tower of theory. It was born from sleepless nights, from panic attacks disguised as "urgent meetings," from 4-7-8 breaths taken in a hospital bathroom before walking in to see a patient.

And above all, it was born from you. From the letters, the messages, the looks in my office that said, *"I thought I was the only one."* That's why this is not a manual that demands you "stop thinking." It's a hand held out for when fear screams louder than your faith. I cannot promise it will disappear. But I can promise this: You are not broken. You are learning to live with an alarm system that cares too much.

Read this book as if it were a conversation. Not all at once.
Return to Chapter 4 when panic rises.
Pause at Chapter 7 if you feel you can't go on alone.
Underline, tear the pages, cry over them.

Because this book is not mine. It is ours. And if today you only have the strength to read this introduction... You are already on your way.

With hope and hands held out,
Dr. Alphonse Semsch

BOOK 1: "WHEN FEAR TAKES OVER"
A Practical Guide to Understanding Your Anxiety and Taking Back Control of Your Life

PART 1
Understanding What's Happening to You (Without the Fluff)

Chapter 1:
"You're Not Crazy, You're Wounded"

A few years ago, a woman walked into my office with trembling hands. Not from the cold—it was summer in Texas—but because she hadn't slept for three nights. "Doctor," she said with a broken voice, "I think I'm going crazy. My mind won't stop. I feel like something bad is going to happen... and I don't know what it is, but I can feel it in my bones."

She looked at me with pleading eyes, as if I held the key to silencing that internal noise. And in that moment, I didn't give her a prescription. I gave her something more urgent: relief from judgment. "Ma'am," I told her, "You're not crazy. You're wounded. And there's a huge difference between the two."

Because madness isolates. But a wound... a wound makes us human.

Anxiety is not a whim. It's not "overthinking." It's the silent cry of a soul that has been on guard for too long. Maybe because of a grief that hasn't been wept. A betrayal left unspoken. Years of saying "I'm fine" while everything inside was falling apart. Maybe from carrying the world, thinking no one else could hold it.

Your body is not betraying you. Your mind is not failing you. What's happening is that your alarm system—that marvelous gift that has kept you alive—is now sounding even when there is no fire. And that is not your fault. It's a signal. A call for help disguised as panic.

On my journey as a doctor, as a researcher, and above all as a human being who has also known fear, I've learned this: God did not give you a spirit of fear, but He did give you a nervous system that sometimes needs to be reconnected with calm.

And that reconnection begins with a radical decision: **Stop fighting yourself.**

You don't need to "stop thinking."
You don't need to "be stronger."
You just need compassion.

The same compassion you would give to a frightened child, to a friend in crisis... but now, given to you.

Practical Exercise: The Self-Forgiveness Ritual

Tonight, before going to sleep, sit in silence for five minutes. Place one hand on your chest and say softly (or in your mind):

"Forgive me for believing I had to do everything alone.
Forgive me for judging myself for feeling afraid.
Today, I choose to take care of you. Not because you're already okay... but because you're already worthy."

Do this for three nights in a row. Don't expect miracles. Just presence.

Pocket Mantra to Carry with You:

"You are not broken. You are in process. And even the cracks let the light in."

Brief Testimonial (Anonymous):

"After years of therapy, medication, and 'well-intentioned advice,' it was a phrase from Dr. Semsch that changed me: 'Your anxiety is not your enemy. It's the part of you that never stopped fighting for you.' I cried like I hadn't cried in years. For the first time, I felt... accompanied."

Mike, age 29

This book is not a manual to "eliminate" anxiety. It is an invitation to reconcile with it... so that, little by little, it stops being in control... and you reclaim your place.

Because you are not your fear.
You are the awareness that observes it.
And that awareness... is already freedom.

Quick Access Guide – Chapter 1

When you feel that "I'm going crazy" or "This isn't normal."

Remember this (in 10 seconds):

> **"I am not crazy. I am wounded. And wounds heal with care, not criticism."**

Do this now (in less than 1 minute):
1. Stop the judgment: Say softly, "This is anxiety, not weakness."
2. Connect with your body: Place one hand on your chest, the other on your abdomen. Feel your warmth.
3. Breathe with purpose: Inhale for 4 seconds → hold for 2 → exhale slowly for 6 seconds. Repeat 3 times.

Now, ask yourself with tenderness:

> **"What part of me needs to feel safe today?"**
> (Don't look for the perfect answer.) (Just listen.)

If you're alone and the fear tightens:
- Send yourself a text message with this phrase:

> **"I am here with you. You are not alone."**

- Call a support line (see Chapter 9) or open a guided breathing app.

To carry with you:

"My anxiety does not define me. My courage does."

With hope, faith, and hands held out.

Chapter 2:
"Worrying Is Not the Same as Drowning in 'What If'"

Recently, a young man told me, *"Doctor, I don't understand. Everyone worries, right? So why do I feel like I'm drowning in my thoughts?"* I replied with an image I often use in my office: *"Worrying is like looking out the window before leaving: Will it rain? Should I take an umbrella?"*

But paralyzing anxiety is like getting stuck at the window, imagining that the sky is going to fall... and that you won't be able to withstand it." There is an abysmal difference between preparing for life and living as if disaster has already struck.

Normal worry is brief, specific, and leads to action: "I have an important meeting. I'll review my notes." "My child has a fever. I'll take him to the doctor."

But clinical anxiety is diffuse, repetitive, and paralyzing: "What if I fail? What if they humiliate me? What if I'm never enough?" "What if something bad happens to someone I love... and it was my fault for not foreseeing it?" It's not that you think more than others.

It's that your mind interprets uncertainty as dangerous... and your body responds as if you were already in danger. And here is the cruelest part: The more you try to control the uncontrollable, the more you lose control over what does depend on you: your breath, your presence, your inner peace.

But there's good news: your anxiety is not your destiny. It's a mental habit... and habits can be retrained.

It's not about eliminating the "what will happen if..." It's about changing your relationship with it. About no longer treating it as a prophecy… and starting to see it as an echo of the past, not a map of the future.

Practical Exercise: The Question That Breaks the Loop

The next time your mind goes into "what will happen if…" mode, stop and ask yourself:

> **"Is this happening now… or only in my imagination?"**

If the answer is "only in my imagination," add:

> **"What if, instead of fighting what doesn't exist, I cared for what *is* here: my breath, my feet on the ground, this moment?"**

Do it every time. Not to stop the thought, but to remind yourself that you are in the present, not in the storm your mind invented.

> Pocket Mantra to Carry with You:
>
> **"Uncertainty is not your enemy. It's the space where faith lives… and freedom."**

Brief Testimonial (Anonymous):

"I spent hours imagining catastrophic scenarios about my work, my health, my family. One day, I wrote down all my 'what ifs…' on a piece of paper. Then, next to them, I wrote: 'Has it ever happened?' The answer was: 'Never.' That day I understood that I wasn't preparing for life… I was running from it."

Daniel, 37 years old

This chapter does not aim to take away your ability to anticipate. On the contrary, it wants to give it back to you without enslaving you. Because life isn't lived in the imagined future... but in the present moment you're breathing in.

Quick Access Guide – Chapter 2

When your mind gets stuck in "What if...?"
Remember this (in 10 seconds):

"My mind is trying to protect me... but not everything it imagines is real."

Do this now (in less than 1 minute):

Stop the loop: Say softly: "This is a projection, not a fact."

Anchor into the present:
- Look around and name:
  - 3 things you see
  - 2 things you hear
  - 1 thing you feel in your body

Breathe with intention: Inhale calm, exhale fiction.

Ask yourself with clarity:

"Is this helping me live... or flee?"

If the thought returns (and it will): Don't fight. Just say:

"Thank you for the warning. I'm already here."

Return to your senses. The present is always waiting for you.

To carry with you:

"I don't need to predict the future to be prepared. I only need to be present."

With hope, faith, and hands held out.

Chapter 3:
"When Anxiety Becomes Your Toxic 'Friend'"

For years, anxiety can seem helpful. It warns you. It prepares you. It keeps you alert. But over time, something changes. It stops being an alarm... and becomes a constant companion. A voice that's always there, whispering: *"You can't trust. You're not ready. Something bad is coming."* And at some point, often without you noticing, that company stops giving you energy... and starts draining your life.

That's when the anxiety stops shouting... and sadness enters in silence. It's not unusual. In fact, it's deeply human. Because when fear becomes chronic, the body wears out. The mind grows tired of fighting shadows. And the heart, little by little, begins to close... not out of coldness, but for protection.

This is where anxiety and depression meet. Not as enemies, but as wounded sisters.

Anxiety says: *"Watch out! Something terrible is going to happen!"*
Depression replies: *"It already happened. And I couldn't stop it."*

And together, they make you believe you're alone... that there's no way out... that you're no longer any use.

But listen closely to this, because it's true: depression is not an absence of faith. It's the sign that you've been carrying too much, for too long, without permission to rest.

In my practice, I've seen so many patients who come in saying: *"Doctor, I don't even have the strength to be afraid anymore."* And in that moment, I don't talk to them about "getting up" or "thinking positively."

I tell them: *"Your soul is asking for a hug... not an order."* This book focuses on anxiety, yes. But it would be irresponsible not to recognize that, for many, fear doesn't end in panic... it ends in emptiness.

And that emptiness deserves to be named. Not to scare you, but so you know: if you feel the light fading, you're not failing. You're calling for help. And that is an act of courage.

In Book 2, "When the Light Goes Out," we will explore that territory in greater depth.

But today, here, I want you to know this: You are not failing because you feel tired. You are being human. And humans need rest, companionship, and hope... not just tools.

Practical Exercise: The Letter to Your "Toxic Friend"

Take a piece of paper and write a letter addressed to your anxiety, as if it were a "friend" who has been with you for a long time. Acknowledge what it tried to do for you:

"Thank you for trying to protect me. For not letting my guard down. For reminding me that life is fragile."

Then, with tenderness but firmness, write:

"But I no longer need to live on alert. Today, I choose to trust... not that nothing bad will happen, but that I will be able to handle whatever comes. You can rest now."

Burn the paper, save it, or let it go to the wind.
It's a symbolic ritual of changing the relationship, not of rejection.

Pocket Mantra to Carry with You:

"I am not alone because I feel empty. I am human. And even the desert blooms... with time and rain."

Brief Testimonial (Anonymous):

13

"I thought my anxiety was my biggest problem. Until one day I woke up and didn't want to get up... not even to prevent a disaster. That's when I understood: it wasn't that I no longer felt fear. It was then that I no longer had hope. And asking for help with that was the bravest thing I've ever done."

Elena, 42 years old

This chapter is not a diagnosis. It's a bridge.

A reminder that emotional suffering rarely comes in separate, sealed compartments. And that recognizing exhaustion... is not surrender. It's the first step toward healing with integrity.

Quick Access Guide – Chapter 3

"When you feel that fear no longer gives you energy... only exhaustion. Remember this" (in 10 seconds):

> ***"I am not broken. I am exhausted. And exhaustion deserves care, not criticism."***

Do this now (in less than 1 minute):

Name what you feel:

> Say softly: ***"I am tired. Not weak. Tired."***

Connect to your breath: Inhale 4 → hold 2 → exhale 6.

Touch yourself gently: Place one hand on your shoulder, as a friend would. Stay there for 30 seconds.

Ask yourself with compassion:

> ***"What do I need today to feel accompanied... even if only by myself?"***

If you feel "like you can't go on": You're not alone. Call a crisis line (see Chapter 9).

Send this message to someone you trust:

"Today is a hard day for me. I don't need solutions. I just need to know you're there."

To carry with you:

"My tiredness is not failure. It's a sign that I have been fighting... and I deserve rest."

With hope, faith, and hands held out.

PART 2
Your Basic Toolbox

Chapter 4:
"Breathing Is Not Optional"

Years ago, in the emergency room of a rural hospital, I had to treat a young man having a panic attack so intense that he believed he was dying. His pulse was racing, he was sweating cold, and he could barely speak.

I took his hand and said, *"We're not going to talk. We're just going to breathe together."* I inhaled deeply through my nose... and exhaled slowly through my mouth. He mimicked me. Once. Twice. On the fifth breath, his shoulders lowered. On the seventh, his eyes welled with tears. And on the tenth, he whispered to me: *"No one had ever taught me I could do this... just with my breath."*

Dear reader: Your breath is your first medicine. It costs nothing. It doesn't require a prescription. And it's with you in every moment... even when you feel everything falling apart.

And yet, in the midst of panic, we forget the most basic thing: that inhaling is receiving... and exhaling is releasing.

The technique you'll learn here —the 4-7-8 breath— is not magical. But it is scientific, ancient, and profoundly human. Dr. Andrew Weil popularized it, but its roots lie in the conscious breathing traditions of yoga and contemplative prayer.

And its power lies in something simple: it activates your parasympathetic nervous system, the one that tells your body, "You are safe." "You can rest."

When anxiety screams, breath responds in silence. And it wins.

Practical Exercise: The 4-7-8 Breath (Your Anchor in the Storm)

How to do it:
1. Sit or lie down comfortably.
2. Place the tip of your tongue against the roof of your mouth, behind your front teeth (and leave it there for the entire exercise).
3. Exhale completely through your mouth, making a soft "whoosh" sound.
4. Close your mouth and inhale silently through your nose while mentally counting to 4.
5. Hold the air in your lungs while counting to 7.
6. Exhale completely through your mouth (with the "whoosh" sound) while counting to 8.
7. That is one breath. Repeat the cycle 4 times.

When to use it:
- Upon waking (to start the day calmly).
- Before sleep (to calm a racing mind).
- During a panic attack (as an emergency anchor).
- Before a difficult conversation, a meeting, or an important decision.

Important tip:

Don't wait until you're in crisis to practice it. Do it twice a day, like brushing your teeth. This way, when fear arrives, your body will already know the way back to calm.

Pocket Mantra to Carry with You:

"Every exhalation is an opportunity to let go of what no longer serves you."

Brief Testimonial (Anonymous):

"I used to take pills to sleep. Until I learned the 4-7-8 breath. The first night I tried it was hard! By the fifth night, I realized I hadn't taken any more pills... and for the first time in years, I wasn't afraid of not sleeping. That changed everything."

Raúl, 51 years old

This is not just a "relaxation trick."

It is an act of trust in your body.

Because in a world that tells you must control everything, breathing reminds you:

> **"You already have within you what you need to come home... to yourself."**

Quick Access Guide – Chapter 4

When you feel panic rising or your mind won't stop:

Remember this (in 10 seconds):

> **"My breath is my anchor. I don't need to control the fear... I just need to return to my breath."**

Do this now (in less than 2 minutes):
1. Sit down. Close your eyes if you can. Focus on your forehead.
2. Exhale all the air (gently).
3. Inhale 4 → hold 7 → exhale 8.
4. Repeat 4 times. (If 7 seconds is too long, use 4-4-6. What matters is that the exhalation is longer than the inhalation.)

Ask yourself calmly:

"What part of my body needs oxygen... and permission to rest?"

If you're in public and can't close your eyes:
1. Breathe slowly through your nose, exhale through your mouth as if softly blowing out a candle.
2. Count silently. No one will notice... but you will.

To carry with you:

"Inhale calm. Exhale fear. One breath at a time."

With hope, faith, and hands held out.

Chapter 5:
"For the Loop-Playing Mind"
(Ruminating Thoughts)

Have you ever felt like your mind is like a scratched record? Over and over, it repeats the same phrase, the same image, the same "what if...?" It doesn't matter how many times you try to stop it. It doesn't matter how much you tell yourself, "Enough!" The loop continues. Spinning. Speeding up. Draining you.

I've been there. And I've been with hundreds of patients who come to my office with eyes tired from so much thinking that leads nowhere. I tell them something that sounds simple, but is revolutionary: **"Your mind doesn't need more control. It needs an anchor."**

Because obsessive thoughts don't stop with more thoughts. They are interrupted by physical presence. With touch. With movement. With the body reminding the mind: **"You are here. Not in the future. Not in the past. Here."**

This chapter teaches you a powerful tool: cognitive interruption through physical anchors. It's not magic. It's neuroscience with soul. And it works because the nervous system cannot be in panic and in contact with the present at the same time.

Practical Exercise: The "Here and Now" Ritual

When you notice your mind entering a loop (repeating fears, criticisms, or catastrophic scenarios), do this:
1. Stop.
   Don't fight the thought. Just say silently: "Ah, there you are again."
2. Activate a physical anchor (choose one that works for you):

- Touch: Gently rub your palms together for 10 seconds. Feel the warmth, the texture, the pressure.
- Movement: Stand up and take three slow steps. Feel every part of your foot touching the floor.
- Temperature: Take a glass of cold water and hold it. Feel the cold in your hands.
- Sound: Say one simple word out loud: "Peace," "Here," or "Enough." Listen to your own voice.

3. Return to the present with a question:

**"What do I need at this very moment to feel safe?"
(Don't search for a big answer.) Sometimes it's just: "To breathe." Or: "To drink water."**

Do this every time the loop returns. It's not about eliminating the thought… but about changing your relationship with it. About watching it pass… without getting on the train.

Pocket Mantra to Carry with You:

"I don't have to stop the noise. I just have to choose not to follow it."

Brief Testimonial (Anonymous):

"I would spend hours imagining I had offended someone or made a mistake at work. One day, my therapist told me, 'Every time the thought returns, touch your bracelet.' I did it. And with time, the thought lost its power. It didn't disappear… but it no longer kidnapped me."

Sofía, 28 years old

This exercise is not about "thinking less." It's about **living more**. Because while your mind spins in circles, life goes on… and it's waiting for you in the present, in your hands, in your breath.

Quick Access Guide – Chapter 5

When your mind gets stuck in a repetitive thought.
Remember this (in 10 seconds):

> *"A thought is not a command. It's just a visitor."*

Do this now (in less than 1 minute):

- Acknowledge the loop: Say to yourself, "This is a pattern, not the truth."
- Activate a physical anchor:
    1. Rub your hands together
    2. Touch something with texture (fabric, a stone, your clothing)
    3. Take a sip of cold water
    4. Say softly: "I am here. I am safe."
- Ask yourself clearly:

> *"Does this thought bring me closer to life... or pull me away from it?"*

- If the thought returns (and it will):
    - Don't get frustrated. Just repeat the anchor.
    - Every time you do this, you are retraining your brain.

To carry with you:

> *"My body is my refuge. My mind is just a passing cloud."*

With hope, faith, and hands held out.

Chapter 6:
"The Power of a Minimal Routine"

Not long ago, a man came to my office and told me in a low voice, *"Doctor, I don't even wash my face anymore. It's not that I don't want to... It's that I feel like it's not worth it."*

I didn't tell him to "get up and act." I didn't tell him that "everything gets better with effort." Because when someone is in that place, words of encouragement sound like stones.

Instead, I asked: *"What is the smallest thing you could do today... just to remind yourself that you are alive?"* He looked at me, surprised. And after a silence, he whispered: *"Maybe... open the curtain."*

That morning, he opened the curtain. He let the light in. And even though he didn't wash his face... he saw himself in the mirror for the first time in days.

Dear reader: This chapter is not for those who have energy to spare. It is for those who barely have the strength to breathe... but still want a thread of hope that doesn't demand heroics. Because depression, even when it follows anxiety, is not laziness.

It is soul exhaustion.

And it is not cured with orders, but with minimal rituals of care. A minimal routine is not a to-do list.

It is an act of love toward yourself, however small.
• Brush your teeth.
• Drink a glass of water when you wake up.
• Step into the sun for five minutes.
• Say your name out loud: "I am [your name]. I am here."

These gestures do not "fix" depression. But they break the spell of isolation. And they remind you of something essential: You are still present. And while you are present, there is a possibility.

Practical Exercise: Your Daily Minimal Ritual

Your Daily Minimal Ritual
1. Choose ONE single gesture you can do every day, no matter how you feel. It should be so simple that you can do it even on your worst day. Examples:
    - Sit for 2 minutes next to a window.
    - Play a song you liked as a child.
    - Write one word on a piece of paper: "Today."
2. Do it at the same time each day, like an appointment with yourself.
3. Don't judge it. It doesn't matter if you do it "right." Only that you show up.
4. Afterwards, say silently:
   "I am here. And that is already enough."

Do this for 7 days in a row.

Don't expect a miracle. But notice: Do you feel a little less invisible?

Pocket Mantra to Carry with You:

"I don't need to do a lot to be worthy. I just need to be here."

Brief Testimonial (Anonymous):

"For months, I didn't leave my bed except to go to the bathroom. One day, I decided I would at least put on clean socks. It seems silly, but it was the first day in weeks I felt... human. From there, little by little, I came back."

Javier, 33 years old

This chapter doesn't ask you to run. It only asks you to take a step... even if it's in the same place.

Because sometimes, the most revolutionary act is not achieving something... but reminding yourself that you deserve to be cared for... even by yourself.

Quick Access Guide – Chapter 6

When you feel "I can't do anything":
Remember this (in 10 seconds):

"I don't need motivation. I just need a small gesture of care."

- Do this now (in less than 1 minute):
  Choose a small gesture:
  1. Drink a sip of water
  2. Open a window
  3. Touch your arm gently and say: "I am with you"
     - Do it slowly. With intention.
     - Don't add anything else. Just that.

Ask yourself tenderly:
"What do I need today to feel a little less invisible?"

If you can't do anything today:
- Take one conscious breath.
- That already counts. You are already taking care of yourself.

To carry with you:
"My worth does not depend on what I do. It depends on the fact that I exist."

With hope, faith, and hands held out.

Chapter 7
"When to Seek Professional Help?"

Years ago, a patient told me with shame: *"Doctor, I've tried everything: breathing, meditation, reading books... but I'm still the same. Does that mean I'm a lost cause?"*

I answered with a question: *"If you had a serious infection, would you feel like a failure for needing antibiotics?"*

He looked at me, surprised. And then, with tears in his eyes, he shook his head.

Dear reader: Asking for help is not a sign of weakness. It's a sign of emotional intelligence. Because recognizing you need support doesn't mean you've failed... it means you respect yourself enough not to keep suffering alone.

Anxiety is a human response.

But when it becomes chronic, intense, or interferes with your daily life, it is no longer just an emotional state: it is a treatable medical condition.

And just like with diabetes, hypertension, or a fracture, there are times when you need a specialist.

It's not about "stopping the fight." It's about fighting with the right tools.

Clear Signs (Without Alarmism) That It's Time to Seek Professional Help: *(You can check them off if you wish)*

☑ Your anxiety lasts more than two weeks and doesn't improve with self-care techniques.

☑ You avoid important situations (work, family, social outings) due to fear.

☑ You have recurring panic attacks (palpitations, shortness of breath, dizziness, fear of dying or losing your mind).

☑ Your sleep, appetite, or energy levels are persistently disrupted.

☑ You feel that life no longer has meaning, or you've had thoughts that "it would be better if I weren't here."

☑ You've tried practical tools… but the suffering remains overwhelming.

If you recognize one or more of these signs, don't punish yourself. Celebrate that your intuition is speaking to you. **And listen to it.**

Practical Exercise: The First Step Without Pressure

You don't need to "decide today" if you're going to therapy.

You only need to open the door. Do this:
1. Look for a trusted resource (see Chapter 9): a support hotline, a therapist directory, a community center.
2. Call or send a message saying only this:

"I'd like information about support for anxiety."

3. Don't force yourself to commit. Just received the information.
4. Save it. You can use it today… or in a month. But you won't be alone in the decision anymore.

This small gesture—a call, a message—is already an act of courage. Because it breaks the isolation, which is where anxiety grows strongest.

Pocket Mantra to Carry With You:
"Asking for help is not giving up. It is choosing to heal with companionship."

Brief Testimonial (Anonymous):

"I used to think therapy was for 'crazy people.' Until one day, after a panic attack in the supermarket, I called a support line. The voice on the other end didn't judge me. They just said: 'You're doing the right thing.' That call was the beginning of my recovery."

Camila, 26 years old

This chapter does not tell you, "You must go to a therapist."

It tells you: "You have the right not to carry this weight alone."

And that, on the path to calm, there is no shame in asking for a hand... only humanity.

Quick Access Guide – Chapter 7

When you feel "I can't do this alone anymore."
Remember this (in 10 seconds):

"Needing help is not failure. It is wisdom."

Do this now (in less than 2 minutes):
1. **Acknowledge a sign:** Is your anxiety interfering with your life?
2. Save a resource: Write down the number of a support line (see Chapter 9).
3. Send a simple message:

"I need guidance about anxiety."

4. Ask yourself honestly:

"Am I suffering more than necessary... just because I don't want to 'bother' anyone?"

5. If you fear judgment:
    - Remember: professionals don't see you as a "case." They see you as a person who is struggling.
    - The first session is not a commitment. It's a conversation.

To carry with you:

"I don't need to be on the edge of the cliff to deserve help. I only need to be human."

With hope, faith, and hands held out.

PART 3
How to Support Someone You Love.

Chapter 8
"What to Say (and What NOT to Say)"

Not long ago, a mother came to my office in despair: *"Doctor, my daughter has anxiety. I tell her: 'Cheer up!', 'Think positive!', 'Others have worse problems!'... but she just closes up more. What am I doing wrong?"*

I took her hands and told her tenderly, *"You're not doing anything wrong. You're just trying to put out a fire... with words that sound like wind."* Because when someone is in the midst of anxiety, they don't need solutions. They need to feel accompanied. They don't need to be told that *"everything will be okay."* They need to be told: *"I'm here, even if I don't understand."*

In my years as a doctor, I've seen that the greatest relief for someone who is suffering doesn't come from perfect phrases... it comes from compassionate silences, from gestures that say: *"You're not alone."*

This chapter is not a rigid script. It's an invitation to replace the impulse to fix... with the courage to be present.

What to say? (words that heal):
- ✓ "I am here with you." (It doesn't promise a cure, but it offers companionship.)
- ✓ "You don't have to explain everything. Just breathe." (It relieves the pressure to "justify" their anxiety.)
- ✓ "What do you need right now? Silence? A distraction? Just someone to listen?" (It gives control in a moment of internal chaos.)
- ✓ "Thank you for trusting me." (It validates their courage in opening up.)
- ✓ "You are not crazy. You are wounded. And that can heal." (It breaks the stigma with tenderness.)

What NOT to say (even if you mean well):

✘ "Just relax!"
→ Anxiety doesn't turn off with commands. It sounds like: "Your suffering is annoying."

✘ "Think positive."
→ Minimizes their experience. Like telling someone with a fever: "Just imagine you're cool."

✘ "Others have worse problems."
→ Pain is not a competition. This only creates guilt.

✘ "It will pass."
→ Even if it's true, in the moment of panic, it sounds like: "Your pain doesn't matter right now."

✘ "Why don't you exercise/pray/go to therapy?"
→ Even if well-intentioned, it sounds like criticism, not support.

Practical Exercise: Listening Without Rescuing.

The next time someone close to you talks about their anxiety:
1. Don't interrupt to give advice.
2. Maintain eye contact (if comfortable) or sit nearby in silence.
3. Respond with short, validating phrases:
    - "That sounds really hard."
    - "Thank you for telling me."
    - "You're not alone in this."
4. Ask only this:

"Do you want me to listen… or do you want us to look for a solution together?"

Sometimes, the most powerful thing you can do is nothing... except be there.

Pocket Mantra to Carry with You:

"I don't need to fix their pain. I only need to honor it with my presence."

Brief Testimonial (Anonymous):

"My husband used to tell me: 'Stop overthinking!' Until one day, in the middle of a panic attack, he just hugged me and said: 'You don't have to talk. I'm just here.' That day, for the first time, I didn't feel like a burden."

Lucía, 31 years old

Supporting someone with anxiety does not require being a therapist. It only requires humility, patience, and the courage not to turn away from another's pain.

Because sometimes, healing isn't found in words... but in the silent certainty that someone chose to stay.

Quick Access Guide – Chapter 8

When someone you love is in an anxiety crisis.
Remember this (in 10 seconds):

"I am not their savior. I am their companion on the journey."

Do this now (in less than 1 minute):
1. Sit nearby. Don't speak immediately.
2. Say softly: "I'm here. You're not alone."

3. Ask: "Would you prefer I talk… or just stay with you?"

Avoid at all costs:
- Minimizing ("It's not that bad")
- Comparing ("Something worse happened to me")
- Pressuring ("You have to get over it")

If you don't know what to do:
- Offer a glass of water.
- Walk with them in silence.
- Breathe with them.

(Physical presence soothes more than a thousand words.)

To carry with you:

"Your loved one doesn't need solutions. They only need to know they're not alone."

Anxiety is not cured with perfect words. It is calmed by hands that don't let go, gazes that don't turn away, and hearts that say: 'I'm not here to fix you, or to judge you… I'm here because I love you.'

With hope, faith, and hands held out.

Chapter 9
"Resources and Crisis Lines"

Dear reader,

If you have made it this far, you have already taken a brave step.
You have sought understanding.
You have practiced tools.
You have considered asking for help.
And now, this final chapter is not just a list.
It's an embrace in the form of information.

Because sometimes, in the middle of the storm, the most urgent thing is not to understand why... but to know where to find a hand that will hold you.

The resources you will find below have been verified at the time of publication.

But remember: if today you feel like you can't go on, don't wait until you "deserve" help. You deserve it simply because you exist.

Free and Confidential Crisis Lines
📞 United States
- 988 Suicide & Crisis Lifeline Call or text 988 (24/7, available in Spanish and English). Also available via online chat at 988lifeline.
- Crisis Text Line
  Text "HOME" to 741741 (available in Spanish).

📞 Mexico
- Línea de la Vida (National): 800 911 2000. The official, free government line for anxiety, depression, and substance use crises (24/7).
- UNAM Psychology Line: 55 5025 0855.

- SAPTEL (Psychological Help): 55 5259 8121. Available 24/7.

📞 Spain
- Línea 024 (Suicide Prevention): 024. Free, confidential, and available 24/7.
- Teléfono de la Esperanza: 717 003 717. You can also call the regional number (e.g., Madrid: 91 459 00 50).
- Emergencies: 112.

📞 Argentina
- Centro de Asistencia al Suicida (CAS): 135 (free line from the Capital and Greater Buenos Aires area) or (011) 5275-1135 (from anywhere in the country).
- National Mental Health Line: 0800 999 0091. Free and confidential service from the Ministry of Health.

📞 Colombia
- Línea 106: "The Power of Being Heard". The main mental health line in Bogotá and several regions.
- Línea Púrpura (Women Only): 01 8000 112 137 or WhatsApp 300 755 1846.
- National Mental Health Line: Varies by department (e.g., Antioquia: 444 44 48).

⚠ Important Note:
If you find yourself in a dangerous situation or know someone who is, act immediately. This could be a medical emergency; always call your local emergency number (such as 911 in the Americas or 112 in Europe).

Useful Applications
- Sanar Ansiedad (iOS / Android) – Breathing exercises, grounding techniques, and mood tracking. In Spanish.
- Calm or Headspace – Guided meditations, sleep stories, and mindfulness exercises.
- MindShift CBT – Based on cognitive behavioral therapy, designed for anxiety in young people and adults.
- 7 Cups – Free chat with trained volunteers for emotional support (available in Spanish).

Where to Find Affordable Therapy:
- Community Mental Health Centers: In the U.S., search on Findatreatment.
- University Clinics: Many offer low-cost therapy with supervised graduate students.
- Psychologists in Training: Sites like Open Path Collective (U.S.)
- Support Groups: Organizations like the Anxiety and Depression Association of America (ADAA) offer listings of local and virtual groups.
- Psychology Today (Directory): It is the world's largest directory. It allows you to filter by country, city, and, most importantly, it has a "Sliding Scale" or "Fees" filter to find private therapists who accept reduced-fee payments.

Complementary Books (Recommended from the Heart)
- "The Power of Now" – Eckhart Tolle
- "Anxiety Free: Unravel Your Fears Before They Unravel You" – Dr. Robert L. Leahy
- "When the Light Goes Out" – Dr. Alphonse Semsch (your next step if depression is also present)

Practical Exercise: Your Emotional Emergency Plan

Take 10 minutes today to create your "Emotional Emergency Kit":
1. Save in your contacts:
    - A local crisis line
    - The name of a trusted friend (with a note: "Call if I feel alone")

2. Create a folder on your phone called "Resources for Me" containing:
    - Links to breathing apps
    - Key phrases from this book
    - A photo that brings you peace

3. Write on a physical card (and keep it in your wallet):

> "I don't have to solve everything right now. I just need the next step. And I am willing to ask for help."

This kit is not for "when I feel bad." It's to remind you that you are never alone... even in your worst moment.

Key Phrase to Close This Book:

"You don't need to see the whole staircase. Just take the first step."

Brief Testimonial (Anonymous):

"One night, I couldn't take it anymore. I opened this book, called 988, and a calm voice told me: 'Thank you for calling. You are safe now.' That call didn't cure me... but it gave me the time I needed to heal."

David, 24 years old

This book ends here... but your journey has just begun. And as you walk, remember: Fear may be in charge for a while... but you are the one who decides whether to keep listening to it... or to start living.

Quick Access Guide – Chapter 9

When you need help, NOW!
- In the U.S.: Dial 988 or text "HOME" to 741741
- In another country: Search on Psychology Today.
- You are not bothering anyone. You are not exaggerating.
- Your life matters. Today. Right now. Exactly as you are.

With hope, faith, and hands held out,
Dr. Alphonse Semsch
Physician of spirit, soul, and body

EPILOGUE
"When Fear Is No Longer in Charge... You Start Living Again"

Not long ago, a patient told me: *"Doctor, I don't have panic attacks like before. But I still feel like something is missing. As if, by calming the fear, I had discovered a deeper emptiness."*

I smiled at him with sadness and recognition. Because I have been there, too.

Anxiety, no matter how intense, has energy.
It screams.
It runs.
It plans.
It prepares for the worst.

But when you learn to calm it... sometimes, what remains is not peace. It is silence.

And in that silence, many discover an uncomfortable truth: they weren't just anxious. They were also wounded. Exhausted. Alone.

If while reading this book you have felt that, beyond the fear, there is a heaviness not relieved by breathing or grounding... you are not going backwards. You are going deeper.

And for you, there is another path.

This book has given you tools to slow down, to interrupt the loop, to ask for help without shame. But if today you feel you don't even have the strength to use those tools... if the "what if..." has been replaced by a "what's the point? "... then, "When the Light Goes Out" is written for you.

Because healing is not a straight path. Sometimes, you first calm the storm... and then you learn to build a home in the calm.

You don't need to have "defeated" anxiety to close this book.

You only need to know this: Every time you choose to breathe instead of flee, every time you call someone instead of hiding, every time you read a chapter, even if you didn't believe in it... You were already taking back control of your life.

Fear can visit you.
But it doesn't have to be in charge anymore.

With hope, faith, and hands held out,
Dr. Alphonse Semsch

"Your Voice Counts Too!"
Write your own notes, reflections, intentions, or prayers here.

"Your Voice Counts Too!"
Write your own notes, reflections, intentions, or prayers here.

Bibliography by Chapter – *When Fear Takes Over*

Chapter 1: "You're Not Crazy, You're Wounded"
1. Neuroplasticity and Emotional Healing. Doidge, N. (2015). *The Brain's Way of Healing: Remarkable Discoveries and Recoveries from the Frontiers of Neuroplasticity*. Viking.
2. Trauma and Recovery from a Somatic Perspective. Levine, P. A. (2015). *Trauma and Memory: Brain and Body in a Search for the Living Past*. North Atlantic Books.
3. Emotional Validation and Compassion-Focused Therapy. Neff, K. D. (2011). *Self-Compassion: The Proven Power of Being Kind to Yourself*. William Morrow.
4. Anxiety as an Adaptive Alarm Signal. Sapolsky, R. M. (2017). *Behave: The Biology of Humans at Our Best and Worst*. Penguin Press.
5. Mind-Body Connection in Chronic Stress. van der Kolk, B. A. (2014). *The Body Keeps the Score: Brain, Mind, and Body in the Healing of Trauma*. Viking.

Chapter 2: "Worrying Is Not the Same as Drowning in 'What If'"
1. Differentiation Between Normal Worry and Pathological Anxiety. Borkovec, T. D., Ray, W. J., & Stöber, J. (1998). Worry: A cognitive phenomenon intimately linked to affective, physiological, and interpersonal behavioral processes. *Cognitive Therapy and Research*, 22(6), 561–576.
2. Metacognitive Therapy for Rumination. Wells, A. (2009). *Metacognitive Therapy for Anxiety and Depression*. Guilford Press.
3. Anxiety and Experiential Avoidance. Hayes, S. C., Strosahl, K. D., & Wilson, K. G. (2012). *Acceptance and Commitment Therapy: The Process and Practice of Mindful Change* (2nd ed.). Guilford Press.
4. Neuroscience of Anticipatory Fear. Grupe, D. W., & Nitschke, J. B. (2013). Uncertainty and anticipation in anxiety: an

integrated neurobiological and psychological perspective. *Nature Reviews Neuroscience*, 14(7), 488–501.
5. Mindfulness-Based Interventions for Generalized Anxiety. Roemer, L., & Orsillo, S. M. (2009). *Mindfulness- and Acceptance-Based Behavioral Therapies in Practice*. Guilford Press.

Chapter 3: "When Anxiety Becomes Your Toxic 'Friend'"
1. Anxiety-Depression Comorbidity. Kessler, R. C., Sampson, N. A., Berglund, P., Gruber, M. J., Al-Hamzawi, A., Andrade, L., ... & Wilcox, M. A. (2015). Anxious and non-anxious major depressive disorder in the World Health Organization World Mental Health Surveys. *Epidemiology and Psychiatric Sciences*, 24(3), 210–226.
2. Emotional Exhaustion and Burnout from Chronic Stress. Maslach, C., & Leiter, M. P. (2016). *Burnout: The Cost of Caring*. Malor Books.
3. Self-Criticism and Depression. Gilbert, P. (2010). *The Compassionate Mind*. Constable & Robinson.
4. Emotional Dysregulation in Internalizing Disorders. Mennin, D. S., & Fresco, D. M. (2014). Emotion regulation therapy. In *Handbook of Emotion Regulation* (2nd ed., pp. 469–490). Guilford Press.
5. Reconceptualizing Emotional Fatigue as a Signal of Need. Porges, S. W. (2017). *The Pocket Guide to the Polyvagal Theory: The Transformative Power of Feeling Safe*. W. W. Norton & Company.

Chapter 4: "Breathing Is Not Optional"
1. 4-7-8 Breathing and Autonomic Regulation. Weil, A. (2007). *Breathing: The Master Key to Self-Healing*. Sounds True.
2. Neurophysiology of Breathing and the Parasympathetic Nervous System. Brown, R. P., & Gerbarg, P. L. (2012). *The Healing Power of the Breath*. Shambhala.
3. Breathing and Mindfulness-Based Stress Reduction. Kabat-Zinn, J. (2013). *Full Catastrophe Living: Using the Wisdom of*

Your Body and Mind to Face Stress, Pain, and Illness (Revised ed.). Bantam Books.
   4. Breathing Techniques in Panic Management. Craske, M. G., & Barlow, D. H. (2014). *Mastery of Your Anxiety and Panic: Workbook* (5th ed.). Oxford University Press.
   5. Mind-Body Integration Through Conscious Breathing. Farhi, D. (2004). *The Breathing Book: Good Health and Vitality Through Essential Breath Work*. Holt Paperbacks.

Chapter 5: "For the Loop-Playing Mind (Ruminating Thoughts)"

   1. Cognitive Interruption Therapy and Sensory Anchors. Clark, D. A., & Beck, A. T. (2011). *Cognitive Therapy of Anxiety Disorders: Science and Practice*. Guilford Press.
   2. Neuroscience of Ruminative Thoughts. Nolen-Hoeksema, S., Wisco, B. E., & Lyubomirsky, S. (2008). Rethinking rumination. *Perspectives on Psychological Science*, 3(5), 400–424.
   3. Somatic Interventions for Breaking Mental Loops. Ogden, P., Minton, K., & Pain, C. (2006). *Trauma and the Body: A Sensorimotor Approach to Psychotherapy*. W. W. Norton & Company.
   4. Mindfulness and Disidentification from Thought. Segal, Z. V., Williams, J. M. G., & Teasdale, J. D. (2018). *Mindfulness-Based Cognitive Therapy for Depression* (2nd ed.). Guilford Press.
   5. Neurocognitive Retraining for OCD and Rumination. Abramowitz, J. S. (2018). *Getting Over OCD: A 10-Step Workbook for Taking Back Your Life* (2nd ed.). Guilford Press.

Chapter 6: "The Power of a Minimal Routine"

   1. Behavioral Activation for Depression. Martell, C. R., Dimidjian, S., & Herman-Dunn, R. (2021). *Behavioral Activation for Depression: A Clinician's Guide* (2nd ed.). Guilford Press.

2. Neuroscience of Burnout and Self-Care. McEwen, B. S., & Akil, H. (2020). Revisiting the Stress Concept: Implications for Affective Disorders. *Journal of Neuroscience*, 40(1), 12–21.
3. Daily Rituals and Psychological Well-being. Hobson, N. M., Schroeder, J., Risen, J. L., Xygalatas, D., & Inzlicht, M. (2018). The Psychology of Rituals: An Integrative Review and Process-Based Framework. *Personality and Social Psychology Review*, 22(3), 260–284.
4. Self-Compassion in Times of Low Energy. Germer, C. K., & Neff, K. D. (2019). *Teaching the Mindful Self-Compassion Program: A Guide for Professionals*. Guilford Press.
5. "Small Steps" Approach in Therapy. Kanter, J. W., Manos, R. C., Bowe, W. M., Baruch, D. E., Busch, A. M., & Rusch, L. C. (2010). What is Behavioral Activation? A Review of the Empirical Literature. *Clinical Psychology Review*, 30(6), 608–620.

Chapter 7: "When to Seek Professional Help?"

1. Decision to Seek Therapy and Its Barriers. Andrade, L. H., Alonso, J., Mneimneh, Z., Wells, J. E., Al-Hamzawi, A., Borges, G., ... & Kessler, R. C. (2014). Barriers to mental health treatment: results from the WHO World Mental Health surveys. *Psychological Medicine*, 44(6), 1303–1317.
2. Efficacy of Psychotherapy for Anxiety. Cuijpers, P., Sijbrandij, M., Koole, S. L., Andersson, G., Beekman, A. T., & Reynolds, C. F. (2014). The efficacy of psychotherapy and pharmacotherapy in treating depressive and anxiety disorders: a meta-analysis of direct comparisons. *World Psychiatry*, 13(1), 52–58.
3. Stages of Change Model (Prochaska & DiClemente). Prochaska, J. O., & DiClemente, C. C. (2005). The transtheoretical approach. In J. C. Norcross & M. R. Goldfried (Eds.), *Handbook of psychotherapy integration* (2nd ed., pp. 147–171). Oxford University Press.
4. Psychoeducation on Treatable Mental Health Conditions. Corrigan, P. W., Druss, B. G., & Perlick, D. A. (2014). The Impact of Mental Illness Stigma on Seeking and Participating in Mental Health Care. *Psychological Science in the Public Interest*, 15(2), 37–70.

5. Initial Contact and the Therapeutic Alliance. Norcross, J. C., & Lambert, M. J. (2019). *Psychotherapy relationships that work: Volume 1: Evidence-based therapist contributions* (3rd ed.). Oxford University Press.

Chapter 8: "What to Say (and What NOT to Say)"
1. Social Support and Validating Communication. Maisel, N. C., & Gable, S. L. (2009). The Paradox of Received Social Support: The Importance of Responsiveness. *Psychological Science*, 20(8), 928–932.
2. Active Listening and Presence in Helping Relationships. Rogers, C. R. (1980). *A way of being*. Houghton Mifflin Harcourt.
3. Common Mistakes When Supporting Someone with Anxiety. Holm-Hadulla, R. M., & Koutsoukou-Argyraki, A. (2015). Mental Health of Students in a Globalized World: Prevalence of Complaints and Disorders, Methods and Effectivity of Counseling, Structure of Mental Health Services for Students. *Mental Health & Prevention*, 3(1-2), 1–4.
4. Polyvagal Theory and Relational Safety. Porges, S. W. (2017). *The Pocket Guide to the Polyvagal Theory: The Transformative Power of Feeling Safe*. W. W. Norton & Company.
5. Training for Family Members (Psychoeducational Programs). Lucksted, A., McFarlane, W., Downing, D., & Dixon, L. (2012). Recent Developments in Family Psychoeducation as an Evidence-Based Practice. *Journal of Marital and Family Therapy*, 38(1), 101–121.

Chapter 9: "Resources and Crisis Lines"
1. Effectiveness of Crisis Lines and Suicide Prevention. Gould, M. S., Kalafat, J., Harrismunfakh, J. L., & Kleinman, M. (2007). An evaluation of crisis hotline outcomes. Part 2: Suicidal callers. *Suicide and Life-Threatening Behavior*, 37(3), 338–352.
2. Access to Mental Health and Resource Equity. Wang, P. S., Lane, M., Olfson, M., Pincus, H. A., Wells, K. B., & Kessler, R. C. (2005). Twelve-month use of mental health services in the

United States: results from the National Comorbidity Survey Replication. *Archives of General Psychiatry*, 62(6), 629–640.
3. Technology and Mental Health Interventions (mHealth). Torous, J., & Roberts, L. W. (2017). Needed Innovation in Digital Health and Smartphone Applications for Mental Health: Transparency and Trust. *JAMA Psychiatry*, 74(5), 437–438.
4. Therapy Directories and Finding Professionals. American Psychological Association. (2021). *Finding the Right Therapist for You*. APA Practice Guidelines.
5. Safety Planning and Crisis Prevention. Stanley, B., & Brown, G. K. (2012). Safety planning intervention: a brief intervention to mitigate suicide risk. *Cognitive and Behavioral Practice*, 19(2), 256–264.

About the author:

As a physician, I was trained to heal the human body. As a soul grafted onto new soil, I learned to rebuild a sense of home from the ground up.

As a researcher, I came to see data not as cold numbers, but as fragile, human stories whispered in the language of science. It was in this space—where empathy meets evidence—that our work was honored on a global stage. The recognition we received was never about volume; it was about reverence. Reverence for the lived experiences hidden within every data point, and the profound trust placed in us to honor them.

My journey has taught me that the most significant breakthroughs do not happen in labs alone. They happen in the human spirit—when we choose to listen deeply, to begin again courageously, and to find meaning even when the path disappears.

I write as Dr. Alphonse Semsch to extend a simple, steadfast belief: You are not defined by your circumstances. You are refined by them.

If you are navigating your own transformation—between who you were and who you are becoming—I am here not as an expert, but as a fellow traveler. Your next chapter is waiting.

Let's turn the page, together.

TEXMERALCOR HEALTH AND RESEARCH GROUP

¡Si este libro te ayudó, tenemos más por venir!

When Fear Takes Over!

Do you feel like your mind never stops? Like you're always on alert, trapped in the "what if...?"? You are not crazy. You are wounded. And that can be healed.

In this book, Dr. Alphonse Semsch, a physician of spirit, soul, and body, offers you real tools—not theories: the 4-7-8 breathing technique, physical anchors, minimal routines, and clear signs for when to ask for help.

Written with clinical tenderness and lived wisdom, this is not a manual to eliminate anxiety... It is a hand held out to help you trust yourself again.

"You don't need to conquer fear. You just need to remember that you are in command."

dralphonsesemsch.com

www.ingramcontent.com/pod-product-compliance
Lightning Source LLC
Chambersburg PA
CBHW050919160426
43194CB00011B/2467